FEDERAL FORCES

CAREERS AS
FEDERAL AGENTS

A CAREER AS AN
ATF AGENT

CYNTHIA A. ROBY

PowerKiDS
press.

Published in 2016 by The Rosen Publishing Group, Inc.
29 East 21st Street, New York, NY 10010

First Edition

Editor: Caitlin McAneney
Book Design: Mickey Harmon

Photo Credits: Cover (ATF agent, truck), Courtesy of the ATF; cover (logo) Color Symphony/ Shutterstock.com; cover, pp. 1, 3–32 (mesh texture) Eky Studio/Shutterstock.com; p. 5 Vesnaandjic/E+/ Getty Images; p. 7 Buyenlarge/Contributor/Archive Photos/Getty Images; p. 9 Courtesy of the Library of Congress; p. 11 Time Life Pictures/Contributor/The LIFE Picture Collection/Getty Images; p. 13 Alex Wong/Staff/Gettty Images News/Getty Images; pp. 15, 17, 21, 23 APImages.com/ASSOCIATED PRESS; p. 11 Time Life Pictures/The LIFE Picture Collection/Getty Images; p. 19 (main) BOB STRONG/ Staff/AFP/Getty Images; p. 19 (inset) BOB PEARSON/Staff/AFP/Getty Images; p. 25 David McNew/ Staff/Getty Images News/Getty Images; p. 27 (man) Ammentorp Photography/Shutterstock.com; p. 27 (background) Songquan Deng/Shutterstock.com; p. 29 Mike Powell/Digital Vision/Getty Images; p. 30 Getty Images/Handout/Getty Images News/Getty Images.

Cataloging-in-Publication Data

Roby, Cynthia A.
A career as an ATF agent / by Cynthia A. Roby.
p. cm. — (Federal forces: careers as federal agents)
Includes index.
ISBN 978-1-4994-1053-2 (pbk.)
ISBN 978-1-4994-1090-7 (6 pack)
ISBN 978-1-4994-1104-1 (library binding)
1. United States. Bureau of Alcohol, Tobacco, and Firearms — Vocational guidance — Juvenile literature. 2. Criminal investigation — Vocational guidance — United States — Juvenile literature. 3. Law enforcement — Vocational guidance — United States — Juvenile literature. I. Title.
HV8144.B87 R63 2016
363.28—d23

Manufactured in the United States of America

CPSIA Compliance Information: Batch #WS15PK: For Further Information contact Rosen Publishing, New York, New York at 1-800-237-9932

Contents

Working Undercover

Three men sit quietly in a parked truck. A car slowly approaches. The driver parks, grabs a bag, and gets out. She inspects the truck's goods: 1,000 cartons of stolen cigarettes. She opens the bag, which is full of money, to make a deal. Suddenly, bright lights flash. Voices yell: "Get down on the ground!" To the men's surprise, the woman isn't buying their stolen goods. She's an ATF agent working undercover to catch them in the act of illegally selling tobacco.

"ATF" stands for "Bureau of Alcohol, Tobacco, Firearms and Explosives." An ATF agent's job is to reduce violent crime and **smuggling**, protect the public, and respond to acts of **terrorism**. Smuggling alcohol, cigarettes, drugs, and explosives are all crimes, but some people are willing to take risks.

Members of ATF teams must train hard to be prepared for raids, or sudden attacks, and dangerous sting operations. A sting operation is a mission designed to trick and catch a person committing a crime.

Prohibition Police

ATF is a federal law enforcement and **regulatory** agency. Its history can be traced back to 1791, when the first U.S. tax laws on alcohol and tobacco were put in place. The agency fought many violent crimes between 1920 and 1933. At that time, it was known as the **Prohibition** Unit, which was a branch of the Bureau of Internal **Revenue**.

The Prohibition Unit was the federal law enforcement agency formed to enforce the National Prohibition Act of 1919. Its function was to stop the sale and use of alcohol. Prohibition agents were assigned to break up illegal **bootlegging** rings. These agents were well-known because they raided nightclubs and other establishments. This work was dangerous, and Prohibition laws were difficult to enforce.

The Untouchables

The gangster Al Capone once ruled Chicago, Illinois. Known as Scarface, Capone became famous as the leader of Chicago's mafia—an organized crime ring—during the Prohibition era. He and his brothers, Frank and Ralph, were a great challenge for government and police departments. Yet they couldn't escape special agent Eliot Ness and his team. Ness's team, called "the Untouchables," finally broke down Capone's bootlegging empire. Capone was charged on more than 5,000 Prohibition **violations** and served more than seven years in jail.

When Prohibition agents seized alcohol, they often poured it into the sewers in front of the nightclubs they raided.

In spite of strict Prohibition laws, people and businesses still wanted alcohol. This caused the number of bootleggers to increase. Some people even made alcohol in their home. The unlawful distribution, or supplying, of alcohol was out of control. Prohibition failed in 1933, when the country was deep into the Great Depression and needed revenue from alcohol.

The Federal Alcohol Administration (FAA) and Alcohol Tax Unit (ATU) were created to take over regulation of alcohol sales. In 1941, the ATU also took over enforcement of the Federal Firearms Act.

On July 1, 1972, the Bureau of Alcohol, Tobacco and Firearms was established. In 2002, the government shifted the ATF from the Department of the Treasury to the Department of Justice. The agency's name became the Bureau of Alcohol, Tobacco, Firearms and Explosives.

In this 1930 photograph, Prohibition administrator Ames Woodcock stands to the left with a sign that tells suspected bootleggers to stop their cars for inspection.

The Best Prohibition Agent

Isador "Izzy" Einstein didn't *look* like a threat to criminals. He was a Prohibition enforcement agent who applied for the job because his job at the post office was a bit boring. Short and overweight, Izzy walked with a lean and never carried a gun. Izzy was also the best Prohibition agent around.

Izzy's greatest trick was using clever disguises and fake personalities to mask his identity. He spoke Polish, German, Yiddish, Bohemian, Hungarian, and a bit of Italian. In fact, every day he would dress and speak differently and then enter an illegal drinking establishment. He would order a drink. When it came, he'd slap handcuffs on the unlucky bartender and say, "There's sad news here. You're under arrest." He used to bet that he could catch a bootlegger in only half an hour.

Izzy Einstein is shown in the top picture to the right and the bottom picture to the left, alongside fellow Prohibition agent Moe Smith. They arrested 4,932 bartenders and bootleggers between 1920 and 1925, thanks to their great disguises.

At the Crime Scene

If a crime is committed that involves explosives, firearms, **arson**, tobacco, or alcohol, ATF agents are on the scene to investigate. An ATF agent's job is to investigate violations of federal laws within the authority of the U.S. Department of Justice.

During an investigation, an agent must interview witnesses and suspects. They sometimes use **surveillance** equipment to catch criminals. They often search for and collect physical evidence at real and potential crime scenes. At times, a team of agents may take part in dangerous raids.

Catching an Arsonist

In 2003, fire officials in the Washington, D.C., area investigated 14 house fires. Because all were similar, ATF agents were called in to lead the investigation. ATF led a task force made up of local police and fire departments. After combing through evidence from each fire scene, debris was taken to a laboratory and identified. The task force was then able to link 50 fires to a fry cook named Thomas Sweatt. He admitted to setting more than 300 other fires over the course of 30 years.

When explosives are involved, ATF special agents work with explosives specialists, explosives enforcement officers, fire investigators, and criminal science specialists. These teams often work with local first responders, such as police and firefighters. ATF agents and their team find and examine evidence, conduct follow-up investigations, and provide statements in court.

ATF agents are called to the scene when explosives are involved.

At a Moment's Notice

The ATF has five special response teams (SRTs). These teams, which were started in 1996, are assigned to the cities of Los Angeles, Detroit, Dallas, Miami, and Washington, D.C. Each team has 160 members. When team members volunteer for a special agent assignment, they must be ready at a moment's notice. During an assignment, special agents may deal with **hostages** and armed suspects who refuse to surrender peacefully.

When SRTs are called out on special missions, they're considered "activated." Certain members with specific training must be present and ready for action. **Tactical** operators are agents trained for combat. Their skills include disarming explosives and other harmful devices, hostage rescue, and entering buildings with skill and secrecy. They use a variety of special tools and weapons to perform their missions.

This ATF special response team is searching for weapons under a house in New Orleans, Louisiana.

Some ATF agents are chosen to train as crisis negotiators on an SRT. Crisis negotiators specialize in handling situations where people are being held against their will. They must deal with suspects who are angry and threatening those around them, especially hostages.

Tactical medics are trained to provide medical support during all types of risky operations, including training operations. These quick responders work in all field division offices and ATF headquarters. Tactical medics are also emergency medical technicians (EMTs), or paramedics.

SRT canines work alongside tactical teams. They're trained to clear buildings and other high-risk areas. The dogs also search for suspects who are hiding and sniff out explosives. The ATF has eight canine teams in its tactical canine program.

A dog's sense of smell may be up to 100 times stronger than a human's. Perhaps that's why K-9 Nanny, a Labrador retriever, can sense nearly 19,000 explosive compounds. Nanny is an explosives detection canine. She received her training from the Puppies Behind Bars program. For this program, inmates—or prisoners—train ATF dogs to respond to commands such as sitting, coming forward, and stopping. Nanny's job is to help ATF agents locate explosives, firearms, and **ammunition**. She and her owner work together each day to keep people safe.

ATF explosive detection canines are paired with a handler. They train together for 10 weeks and work together until the dog retires at around nine years old.

Ready for a Standoff

Special response teams were developed after the 1993 Branch Davidian tragedy in Waco, Texas. The Branch Davidians are a religious group. Suspecting them of weapons violations, ATF agents raided their compound.

During the raid, four agents died in a shootout. A **siege** followed that resulted in a 51-day standoff with ATF and FBI agents. The group's leader, David Koresh, and his followers burned the compound, ending the standoff. Koresh and 81 Branch Davidians died.

ATF agents must be trained as skilled negotiators to be prepared for the next hostage or standoff situation. In 2014, SRT crisis negotiation training took place in an old warehouse in Minnesota's Dakota County. The two-week training presented real-life situations to give ATF agents experience for when hostage situations arise.

The Branch Davidian compound was destroyed in a
fire set on April 19, 1993.

Investigating Acts of Terrorism

On February 26, 1993, a team of ATF agents sifted through piles of broken cement and debris. They were below street level under New York City's World Trade Center (WTC). Their assignment was to uncover the type of explosives that had destroyed four levels of parking garages below the building.

Within the first 24 hours, agents located bits of important evidence. They found pieces of metal that helped identify the van that transported the explosives into the parking garage. This discovery led agents directly to the person who rented the vehicle.

Retired ATF assistant director Malcolm Brady was at the 1993 WTC scene. He explained that sifting through the debris was like putting parts of a puzzle back together to get evidence.

This dump truck is unloading debris from the 1993 World Trade Center explosion. The event was confirmed as being caused by a bomb, and terrorists were arrested.

On April 15, 2013, ATF agents rushed to Boylston Street in Boston. A few hours earlier, two homemade bombs had been set off at the finish line of the Boston Marathon. On hands and knees, agents searched for debris from the explosion. This was the first step in reconstructing the explosive devices.

Two days later, in West, Texas, a fertilizer plant exploded, killing and injuring many people and ruining nearby homes. ATF agents were quickly on the scene to sift through pieces of debris and hold interviews in hopes of solving the case.

Because of advances in technology, agents today need only take a sample of the explosive residue, or remains. Once at the lab, the type of explosive can be identified within minutes.

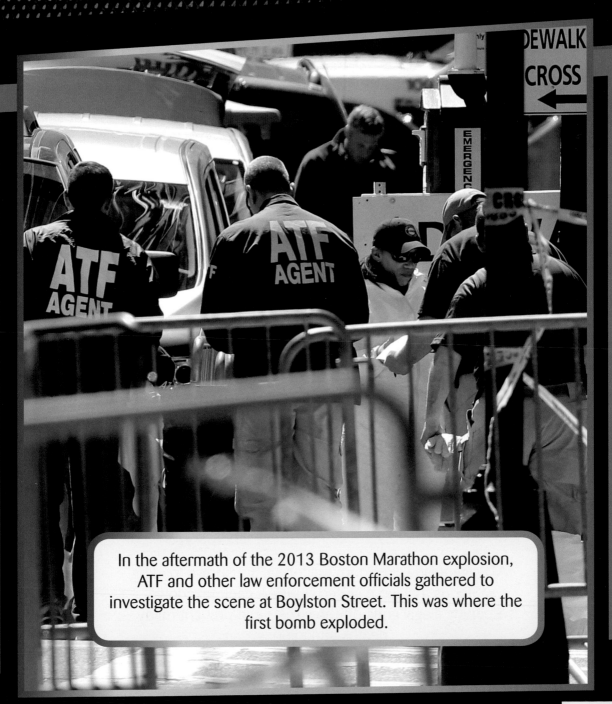

In the aftermath of the 2013 Boston Marathon explosion, ATF and other law enforcement officials gathered to investigate the scene at Boylston Street. This was where the first bomb exploded.

Busting Gunrunners

Conor Claxton, Siobhan Browne, Anthony Smyth, and Martin Mullan—known as the "Florida Four"—were gunrunners, or gun smugglers. In 1998, they plotted to illegally purchase guns and ammunition to send to terrorists in Northern Ireland. There, they would be used against law enforcement and military. What the Florida Four didn't know was that ATF agents and other law enforcement agencies already had them under investigation. The agency tracks every person who buys more than two guns in five days.

ATF agents in Lakewood, California, are shown loading weapons that were seized during a gang takedown. Keeping illegal guns off the streets can prevent many deaths and injuries.

In 1999, authorities seized one of Conor Claxton's shipments. He was then linked to 24 packages that contained 126 firearms, which were all shipped to Northern Ireland. Each of the Florida Four was found guilty and sent to prison.

Stepping into an ATF Career

Jobs with the ATF are challenging but rewarding. The work is tough, and assignments are uncertain. The opportunities, however, are great. The agency **recruits** people from all backgrounds who are ready to make a difference. These recruits must have certain characteristics, such as honesty, good judgment, and loyalty.

ATF applicants, or people who apply, must be U.S. citizens between the ages of 21 and 36. They must submit to drug and lie detector tests and pass a background check, which makes sure they don't have a record of criminal behavior.

Applicants must have a bachelor's, or four-year, degree from a college or university. A degree in the area of criminal justice, law enforcement, political science, or something similar is preferred.

Part of an agent's job is to collect, examine, and document information for use in court. Therefore, they must have the ability to write well.

The job of an ATF special agent requires a lot of physical work. Applicants must be in excellent physical condition because the training is tough.

ATF Preemployment Physical Test

Task Test Scoring Chart
(Scoring for ages 21–29)

Minimum score for the 1.5 mile run

Male: 12 minutes, 16 seconds
Female: 16 minutes, 7 seconds

Minimum push-ups performed in 1 minute

Male: 33   Female: 16

Minimum sit-ups performed in 1 minute

Male: 40   Female: 35

Potential agents have to pass a physical test before they're hired. Some tests measure endurance, or how long an applicant can do a difficult exercise. There are minimum targets for sit-ups and push-ups as well as a 1.5-mile (2.4 km) run. These targets are based on the applicant's age and gender. Applicants must also pass a physical exam given by an authorized government doctor.

ATF agents have to train before they land their job. They go to a two-part program, where they train in self-defense, physical endurance, and using firearms. They also learn how to arrest, interview, and watch possible criminals.

Are You Ready?

Today's ATF grew out of the earliest revenue collectors, undercover Prohibition agents, and inspectors who served throughout the agency's long history. Today, agents conduct surveillance and raids, interview witnesses and suspects, carry out searches, collect evidence, and make arrests. Are you ready to team up with these highly trained men and women?

As federal law enforcement officers, ATF agents' duties often place them in harm's way. They travel often and on a moment's notice. The destination can't be planned. Agents often work outside in all types of weather. However, by controlling alcohol, tobacco, firearms, and explosives in the United States, these agents have the opportunity to save lives every day.

Glossary

ammunition: Bullets, shells, and other things fired by weapons.

arson: The illegal burning of a building or other property.

bootleg: To make or sell alcohol illegally.

hostage: Someone who is being held against their will.

Prohibition: A period of time from 1920 to 1933 in the United States when it was illegal to make or sell alcohol.

recruit: To seek out suitable people and get them to join an organization, company, or the armed forces.

regulatory: To bring under the control of law or authority.

revenue: Money that is collected for public use by a government through taxes.

siege: An operation during which a law enforcement agency surrounds a building and cuts off supplies. The goal is to force an armed suspect or suspects to surrender.

smuggle: To import or export secretly and illegally.

surveillance: The act of watching someone or something closely.

tactical: Relating to a plan or technique designed to reach a desired result.

terrorism: Using violence for political aims.

violation: The act of doing something not allowed by law or rule.

Index

Websites

Due to the changing nature of Internet links, PowerKids Press has developed an online list of websites related to the subject of this book. This site is updated regularly. Please use this link to access the list: www.powerkidslinks.com/fed/atf